This Book Belongs To:

_____

What to do if I Kick the Bucket

A Guide for My Next of Kin

Y. L. Owens

Six One Sixty One Publishers

First published in the United States of America in 2019 by Six One Sixty One Publishers.

Copyright © 2019 by Y. L. Owens

All rights reserved. No part of this book may be reproduced in any form without written permission from the publisher.

ISBN – 9781095584750

Six One Sixty One Publishers
San Antonio, Texas 78259
sixonesixtyone@gmail.com

PREFACE

In 2019, I published the first edition of What To Do If I Kick The Bucket – A Guide For My Next Of Kin and I have to say, the response was amazing and continues to surprise me each and every month. With the addition of the large format workbook size also available, I'm thrilled I've been able to provide people with a little peace of mind. My inspiration for compiling a place for immediate information was simple: Someday I'm going to kick the bucket, and no one knows my passwords!

Some of us kick it so unexpectedly, our social media accounts and online store listings and auctions hang out there in the wind until someone finally figures it out – if they do at all. Our Facebook account is frozen in time because of a long forgotten password not written down since the early aughts.

Very few people have actual wills or advance directives and even if you do have these important items, it's unlikely your daily To Do things are conveniently listed somewhere for a loved one to take care of sooner rather than months later. And really - does your designated agent (i.e. your spouse, your kid, cousin or best friend) know where you keep your will? (Not to mention the key to the side gate.)

This is your chance to put your daily doings all in one place as well as your personal two cents into the planning of that fabulous celebration your loved ones will throw in honor of a life well lived. It's an emotional time for all and a road map from you makes it that much easier.

If you've lost five or ten minutes of sleep wondering who would think to look for your streaming subscriptions and cancel them ASAP or your Amazon Prime account with that upcoming renewal date and automatic debit charge, this book is for you - and them!

These things may seem a bit trivial right now when compared to funeral arrangements and financial matters after your death, but they will need attention.

I've included a section for some family history, your favorite memories and those stories from cherished relatives that are starting to fade. Once those tidbits in time are gone, trust me, they're gone.

Write everything down and tuck it away. There are people who will be grateful you did. It's not on a locked computer with a password no one knows in a file some internet troll might hack.

Once it's done, take a deep breath and get on with your amazing, incredible life!

No one gets out alive,

So you might as well be

organized about it.

Table of Contents

SECTION ONE – PERSONAL INFORMATION

About Me	p.1
Designated Agent	p.21
Do Not Resuscitate Instructions	p.23
Power of Attorney	p.25
Social Security	p.27
Driver's License & Other ID's	p.29
Cell Phone	p.33
Passport	p.35
Organ Donor	p.37
Pet Information	p.39
Military Information	p.45
Safe Deposit Box	p.47

SECTION TWO – LEGAL & MONEY MATTERS

Attorney	p.51
Accountant	p.55
Money Manager	p.57
Broker	p.59

Probate & Estate Administrator	p.61
Document & Key Location	p.63
Bank Accounts	p.73
Credit & Debit Cards	p.77
Retirement Accounts	p.81
Investment Accounts	p.83
Trust Information	p.85
Loans	p.87
Insurance Policies	p.89
Tax Information	p.95

SECTION THREE - UTILITIES

Utilities	p.99
Subscriptions & Memberships	p.103

SECTION FOUR – MEDICAL INFORMATION

Doctors	p.113
Medical History	p.116
Advance Directive/Living Will	p.119

SECTION FIVE – SOCIAL MEDIA ACCOUNTS

Social Media	p.123
Online Stores	p.129
Email Addresses	p.141
Legacy Contacts	p.143

SECTION SIX – FUNERAL ARRANGEMENTS

Funeral Arrangements	p.147

SECTION SEVEN – FAMILY HISTORY

Family History, Stories & Anecdotes	p.161

SECTION EIGHT – HELPFUL INFORMATION

Important Numbers & Websites	p.169
Types of Power of Attorney	p.171
Death Certificate Copies	p.175
Helpful Timeline	p.179

Section One

Personal Information

About Me

Name

First _____

Middle _____

Last _____

Maiden _____

Nickname _____

Legal Name _____

Current Address

_____

_____

_____

_____

Date of Birth

_____

List any past addresses that are memorable such as your childhood address where you grew up, your first apartment or house or any vacation homes you might own etc.

_____

_____

_____

_____

_____

_____

_____

_____

_____

_____

_____

_____

_____

_____

_____

Place of Birth

_____

Gender, Race/Ethnicity

_____

Marital Status

_____

Date of Marriage

_____

Place of Marriage

_____

Date of Divorce/Widowed

_____

Spouse(s) Name(s)

_____

_____

_____

_____

Children

Include their address and phone number and any other important information about them.

Relatives

Close Friends

Education

Elementary/Grade School

_____

_____

Junior/Middle School

_____

_____

High School

_____

_____

Trade School/College/University/Graduate

_____

_____

_____

_____

_____

_____

Occupation(s)

_____
_____
_____
_____
_____

Employer(s)

_____
_____
_____
_____
_____

Union Info/Benefits

_____
_____
_____
_____
_____

Additional Employment Information

Mother's Name, DOB, Place of Birth

_____

_____

_____

_____

_____

_____

_____

Father's Name, DOB, Place of Birth

_____

_____

_____

_____

_____

_____

_____

Maternal Grandparents

_____

_____

_____

_____

_____

Paternal Grandparents

_____

_____

_____

_____

_____

Other Distant Relatives

_____

_____

_____

_____

_____

More About Me

Designated Agent

A Designated Agent is usually the surviving spouse or closest living relative. This is for people who have a Last Will and Testament. If you do not have a will, a probate administrator will be assigned by the court. Responsibilities include paying bills and taxes, making notifications and other arrangements.

My designated agent/executor/best friend/close person is:

_____

_____

Address & Telephone Number

_____

_____

_____

Location of Last Will & Testament

_____

_____

Leave any instructions or additional information about your Designated Agent here:

Do Not Resuscitate Order Instructions

A DNR tells health-care professionals not to perform CPR if your heart or breathing stops and restarting would not result in a meaningful life.

1. Have a **Do-Not-Resuscitate Order** drawn up **BY YOUR DOCTOR** if you so desire. An Out-of-Hospital DNR is signed by your doctor and tells emergency medical personnel not to use certain procedures to resuscitate or revive you. A Directive to Physicians tells your doctor to withhold or withdraw certain life-saving treatment if your doctor certifies that your condition is terminal or irreversible

2. Consider completing an advance directive, including a living will, which specifies wanted and unwanted procedures. You should also consider appointing a health-care proxy to make medical decisions if you become incapacitated.

3. Make sure to give copies of the documents to your doctor and a few family members or friends. Take the documents to the hospital if you are admitted.

I have a DNR

_____ Yes

_____ No

Copies are located:

_____

_____

_____

_____

Power of Attorney

A Power of Attorney (POA) is legal authorization for a designated person to make decisions about another person's property, finances, or medical care.

My Power of Attorney is:

_____

_____

Address & Telephone Number

_____

_____

_____

_____

There are different types of Power of Attorney. Please see page 169 for more information.

Leave any instructions or additional information about your Power of Attorney here:

Social Security Number

My SS# is:

___ ___ ___   ___ ___   ___ ___ ___ ___

Social Security Administration

1-800-772-1213

www.ssa.gov

Register for a free, personal My Social Security account. Receive personalized estimates of future benefits based on your real earnings, see your latest statement, and review your earnings history. Request a replacement Social Security Card and more.

Driver's License & Other ID's

State:

_____

Number:

_____

Expiration:

_____

Organ Donor: (see page 35 for more info)

Yes _____

No   _____

Other ID's:

Cell Phone

Cell Phone Number

_____

Carrier

_____

Passcode To Open Phone

_____

Billing Pass Code (required by some carriers)

_____

Legacy Contact(s) (see page 141 for more information)

_____

_____

_____

_____

_____

Any other pertinent information about your phone:

Passport

Country

_____

Number

_____

Date of Issue/Expiration Date

_____

US Passport Office

1-877-487-2778   www.travel.state.gov

_____
_____
_____
_____

Immigration and Citizenship Information

Organ Donor

I am an organ donor _____

    Living _____

    Deceased _____

I am NOT an organ donor: _____

For information about both living and deceased organ donation: **www.organdonor.gov**

_____

_____

_____

_____

_____

If there are no dogs in Heaven, then when I die, I want to go where they went.

Will Rogers

_____

Pet Information

Person who will take care of my pets:

_____

_____

_____

_____

Dogs: _____ Cats: _____ Birds: _____

List All Other Pets Here:

_____

_____

_____

_____

_____

_____

_____

Veterinarian

Additional Instructions

Old soldiers never die,

they simply fade away.
───────────────────────

Military

Entered Service Date _____

Entered Service Place _____

_____

Service Number _____

Separated From Service Date _____

Separated From Service Place _____

_____

Grade, Rank or Rating _____

Organization and Branch of Service _____

_____

_____

_____

Safe Deposit Box

Bank Name & Address

_____

_____

_____

_____

_____

Box Size _____

Key Location _____

Contents:

_____

_____

_____

_____

_____

_____

_____

Section Two

Legal & Money Matters

Attorney

Name, Address & Telephone Number

_____

_____

_____

_____

_____

_____

I have the following Estate Documents:

_____ Last Will and Testament

_____ Advance Directive/Living Will

_____ Financial Power of Attorney

_____ Living Trust

_____ Other Documents Listed Below

_____

_____

Accountant

Name, Address & Telephone Number

_____

_____

_____

_____

_____

_____

General Tax Information or Instructions

_____

_____

_____

_____

_____

_____

_____

_____

Money Manager

Name, Address & Telephone Number

_____
_____
_____
_____
_____
_____

Accounts and Documents

_____
_____
_____
_____
_____
_____
_____

Broker

Name, Address & Telephone Number

Accounts and Documents

Probate and Estate Administrator

Assigned to the estate by the court when there is no Will and Last Testament.

Name, Address & Telephone Number

_____

_____

_____

_____

_____

Court (& Other) Instructions

_____

_____

_____

_____

_____

_____

Document & Key Location

Will and Last Testament (see page 51 for more information)

_____

_____

_____

_____

_____

Advance Directive/Living Will (see page 119 for more information)

_____

_____

_____

_____

_____

Birth Certificate

Social Security Card

Keys

DNR – DO NOT RESUSCITATE ORDER (see page 23 for more information.)

_____
_____
_____
_____

Wanted & Unwanted Procedures Document

_____
_____
_____
_____
_____

Healthcare Proxy in Case of Incapacitation Document

_____
_____
_____
_____
_____

Life Insurance Policies

Other Financial Documents

Marriage License/ Divorce Decree

_____

_____

_____

_____

_____

Military Discharge Papers

_____

_____

_____

Home Deed

_____

_____

_____

Deed to Burial Property

_____

_____

_____

Letter of Final Instructions/Disposition

_____

_____

_____

Copy of Funeral Arrangements

_____

_____

_____

_____

_____

Miscellaneous Other Things and Their Location

_____

_____

_____

_____

_____

_____

_____

In this world, nothing is certain, except death and taxes.

Benjamin Franklin
───────────────────────

Bank Accounts

Joint accounts and accounts with co-signers should have easy access to the account. If there are no joint owners or co-signers, no one can access the account until a Personal Representative has been approved through the court process and/or the Probate Administrator.

Bank(s)

_____

_____

_____

_____

_____

Branch Contact, Address & Phone Number

_____

_____

_____

_____

Checking Account (s) & Routing Number (s)

_____

_____

_____

_____

_____

_____

_____

Savings Account (s) & Routing Number (s)

_____

_____

_____

_____

_____

_____

_____

Additional Account (s)

Money Market Account(s)

_____

_____

_____

_____

_____

Certificate of Deposit Account(s)

_____

_____

_____

_____

_____

Other Accounts:

_____

_____

_____

_____

_____

Credit and Debit Cards

List your credit card and debit card numbers along with their expiration dates for your Visa, MasterCard, American Express and Discover cards. Remember to update this section each time you receive a new card.

Retirement Accounts

List any retirement accounts such as your 401k, a Traditional IRA, Roth IRA, SEP IRA, Simple IRA or Simple 401k etc.

_____

_____

_____

_____

_____

_____

_____

_____

_____

_____

_____

_____

Investment Accounts

List any investment accounts, rental properties or any other miscellaneous types of income your heirs need to know about here.

_____

_____

_____

_____

_____

_____

_____

_____

_____

_____

_____

Trust Information

List any Family Trust information here. The purpose of a Family Trust is to establish a way for your family to reap direct financial benefits from your estate planning efforts. Your attorney will set one up if you feel your situation deems it necessary.

Loans

List any personal or commercial loans here. Include any loans for which you receive payments and for which you make payments.

Personal Loans

_____

_____

_____

_____

_____

_____

_____

_____

_____

_____

Commercial Loans

Insurance Policies

Medical

_____
_____
_____
_____
_____
_____
_____
_____

Life Insurance

_____
_____
_____

Long Term Care Insurance

Homeowners Insurance

_____
_____
_____
_____

Car Insurance

_____
_____
_____
_____

Burial Insurance

_____
_____
_____
_____
_____

Miscellaneous Other Insurance

Tax Information

List any information about your tax situation here, especially if you do not have an accountant and you do your taxes yourself. Notate the location of your tax returns as they may be helpful to the people handling your estate.

_____

_____

_____

_____

_____

_____

_____

_____

_____

Section Three

Utilities, Subscriptions & Memberships

Utilities

Make a list of regular monthly bills and due dates. Be sure to note if any are on automatic payment plans and how and where to cancel.

Electricity   **Due Date**_____

_____

_____

_____

_____

_____

Gas   **Due Date**_____

_____

_____

_____

_____

_____

Water   **Due Date**_____

_____

_____

_____

_____

_____

Cable   **Due Date**_____

_____

_____

_____

_____

_____

Telephone   **Due Date**_____

_____

_____

_____

_____

_____

Other Utilities

Subscriptions & Memberships

Netflix

Login: _____

PW: _____

Amazon Prime

Login: _____

PW: _____

Hulu

Login: _____

PW: _____

Apple TV

Login: _____

PW: _____

Paramount+

Login: _____

PW: _____

Peacock

Login: _____

PW: _____

Roku

Login: _____

PW: _____

Disney+

Login: _____

PW: _____

HBO Max

Login: _____

PW: _____

_____

Login: _____

PW: _____

_____

Login: _____

PW: _____

_____

Login: _____

PW: _____

_____

Login: _____

PW: _____

_____

Login: _____

PW: _____

_____

Login: _____

PW: _____

_____

Login: _____

PW: _____

_____

Login: _____

PW: _____

_____

Login: _____

PW: _____

_____

Login: _____

PW: _____

Magazines, Journals, Newspapers

Magazines, Journals, Newspapers

Section Four

Medical Information

Medical Information

Primary Care Doctor(s)

_____
_____
_____
_____
_____
_____
_____
_____

Specialist(s)

_____
_____
_____
_____

Medical History

List any important medical information or the location of your medical files.

Advance Directive/Living Will

Living wills and other advance directives are written, legal instructions regarding your preferences for medical care if you are unable to make decisions for yourself. Advance directives guide choices for doctors and caregivers if you're terminally ill, seriously injured, in a coma, in the late stages of dementia or near the end of life.

Each state has different forms and requirements for creating legal documents such as Living Wills and Advance Directives. A form may need to be signed or notarized and you can ask a lawyer to help you with the process but it is generally not necessary. Check online for your state requirements.

Advance directives usually fall into three categories: Living Will, Power of Attorney and Health Care Proxy.

I HAVE AN ADVANCE DIRECTIVE/LIVING WILL

       YES _____ No _____

Location:

_____

Section Five

Social Media Accounts

Email Addresses

Social Media Accounts

Facebook

Password _____

Delete My Account

        Yes _____ No _____

Keep My Account in Memoriam

        Yes _____ No _____

To keep Facebook in Memoriam, go to Settings, General, Manage Account, Modify Your Legacy Content Settings.

Please post this for me as my last post: (Poem, Memorial, Favorite Quote, Photo)

_____

_____

_____

_____

_____

_____

Instagram Password _____

LinkedIn Password _____

Premium Account Yes _____ Needs to be cancelled

Twitter Password _____

Pinterest Password _____

YouTube Password _____

Snapchat Password _____

TikTok Password _____

WhatsApp _____

_____

_____

_____

_____

_____

More Social Media Instructions:

Online Stores

Amazon

Login _____

Password _____

    _____ I have listings that need to be deleted.

    _____ I have listings that might need fulfilment.

Instructions

_____

_____

_____

_____

_____

_____

_____

_____

_____

EBAY

Login _____

Password _____

_____ I have listings that need to be deleted.

_____ I have listings that might need fulfilment.

Instructions

_____
_____
_____
_____
_____
_____
_____
_____
_____
_____
_____
_____

Etsy

Login _____

Password _____

    _____ I have listings that need to be deleted.

    _____ I have listings that might need fulfilment.

Instructions

Shopify

Login _____

Password _____

_____ I have listings that need to be deleted.

_____ I have listings that might need fulfilment.

Instructions

_____
_____
_____
_____
_____
_____
_____
_____
_____
_____
_____
_____
_____
_____

Other Websites and Stores

Login _____

Password _____

_____ I have listings that need to be deleted.

_____ I have listings that might need fulfilment.

Instructions

Other Websites and Stores

_____

Login _____

Password _____

_____ I have listings that need to be deleted.

_____ I have listings that might need fulfilment.

Instructions

_____

_____

_____

_____

_____

_____

_____

_____

_____

Email Accounts

List your email addresses, passwords and/or login instructions.

Legacy Contacts

Facebook and Apple have a Legacy Contact that lets you choose a friend to manage your account and iPhone (15.2 and above) posthumously.

For Facebook, your friend will be able to manage tribute posts on your site, delete your site, accept new friends, and update your profile. Instructions: Settings – Personal Information – Manage Account – Legacy Contact. Follow onscreen instructions from there.

Facebook Legacy Contact

_____

_____

On your iPhone (15.2 or later) – Settings – Tap Your Name at the Top – Password and Security – Scroll to Bottom for Legacy Contact. You can add up to 5 legacy contacts.

iPhone Legacy Contact(s)

_____

_____

Section Six

Funeral Arrangements

Reports of my death

are greatly exaggerated.

Mark Twain

Funeral Arrangements

Date of my death: _____

My age: _____

(Obviously this is for someone else to fill in for future reference.)

My Burial Instructions and Wishes

_____

_____

_____

_____

_____

_____

_____

_____

_____

_____

_____

Cremation Instructions

_____
_____
_____
_____
_____
_____
_____

Religious Ceremony Instructions

_____
_____
_____
_____
_____
_____
_____
_____
_____

Wake Wishes

Music Preferences

My Accomplishments

Don't be shy. There's an obituary to be written and a program for your funeral and/or memorial service. Friends and family will want to acknowledge your achievements and that rockin' wake too! You earned it.

_____

_____

_____

_____

_____

_____

_____

_____

_____

_____

_____

_____

_____

_____

_____

Favorite Memories

Section Seven

Family History

Family History, Stories & Anecdotes

Section Eight

Helpful Information

Important Numbers and Websites

Notify the following credit reporting agencies so no one steals my identity. (You'll need my social security number when you call.)

Equifax – 1-800-685-1111   www.equifax.com

Experian – 1-888-397-3742   www.experian.com

TransUnion – 1-800-888-4213   www.transunion.com

Department of Veteran's Affairs

1-800-827-1000   www.va.gov

Social Security Administration

1-800-772-1213   www.socialsecurity.gov

Types of Power of Attorney

A power of attorney is a legal document that allows a principal to appoint an agent to act for them should they become incapacitated. The agent is expected to place the principal's interests ahead of his or her own, which is why it is important for you and your loved one to pick a trusted individual. There are multiple types of decisions that the agent can be given the power to make, including:

1. Make financial decisions

2. Make gifts of money

3. Make healthcare decisions, including the ability to consent to giving, withholding, or stopping medical treatments, services, or diagnostic procedures. (Note: your loved one can also make a separate "health care power of attorney" to give only this power to another individual.)

4. Recommend a guardian

General Power of Attorney

In this situation, the agent can perform almost any act as the principal, such as opening financial accounts and managing personal finances. A general power of attorney arrangement is terminated when the principal becomes incapacitated, revokes the power of attorney or passes away.

Durable Power of Attorney

This arrangement designates another person to act on the principal's behalf and includes a durable clause that maintains the power of attorney after the principal becomes incapacitated.

Special or Limited Power of Attorney

In this instance, the agent has specific powers limited to a certain area. An example is a power of attorney that grants the agent authority to sell a home or other piece of real estate.

Springing Durable Power of Attorney

In some states, a "springing" power of attorney is available and becomes effective when a specified event occurs such as when the principal becomes incapacitated.

Death Certificate Copies

Reasons to order copies of the death certificate:

- Obtain death benefits through an employer
- Claim insurance benefits
- Claim social security benefits
- Transfer bank accounts and insurance policies
- Cancel subscriptions to services and utilities
- Family history and genealogy
- Miscellaneous legal purposes that arise

Generally, you will need one certified copy of the death certificate for each major asset such as cars, land or bank accounts, insurance and veteran's benefits for which you will need to transfer ownership. Certified copies can be expensive so ask if a non-certified photocopy is allowed or if the company would return the original certified copy to use again later.

____ TOTAL NUMBER OF COPIES FROM THE ITEMS I'VE CHECKED BELOW:

____ Saving's Account Beneficiary

____ Property Ownership

    ____ Residence

    ____ Land

    ____ Car

    ____ Boat

    ____ Rental property

    ____ Other

    ____ Other

____ Insurance Policies

____ Brokerage Accounts, Stocks & Bonds

____ Safe Deposit Box

____ Veterans Benefits

____ Union Benefits

____ IRS - send copy of death certificate with next tax return.

____ Post Office – set up mail forwarding to:

_____

_____

_____

_____

____ My attorney who has my will – see p. 39

____ My Credit Card and Loan Accounts – see p. 67

____ IRA Accounts – see p. 71

____ Treasury Bills

____ 401-K

____ Pension Plans

____ Proof of funeral attendance (some family members might need one to show their employer.)

____ Funeral Home (so they can receive payment)

____ Family Members Records

____ Extra Copies

Helpful Timeline

Immediately:

1. Get a legal pronouncement of death. If no doctor is present, you'll need to contact someone to do this.

   If the person dies at home under hospice care, call the hospice nurse who can declare the death and help facilitate the transport of the body.

   If the person dies at home without hospice care, call 911 and have in hand a do-not-resuscitate document if it exists. Without one, paramedics will generally start emergency procedures and except where permitted to pronounce death, take the person to an emergency room for a doctor to make the declaration.

2. Arrange for transportation of the body. If no autopsy is needed, the body can picked up by a mortuary.

3. Notify the person's doctor or the county coroner.

4. Handle the care of any dependents and pets.

5. Notify close family and friends.

6. Notify the designated agent and/or Power of Attorney who will then take care of the necessary arrangements.

7. Look for written instructions (this book!) but also locate any other files the deceased may have left.

Within a few days:

1. Notify the executor of the will (this can also be the designated agent) and the attorney regarding the probate of the estate.

2. Notify religious, fraternal and civic organizations. It may have burial benefits or conduct funeral services.

3. Call the person's employer and request information about benefits and any pay due. Ask whether there was a life-insurance policy through the company.

4. Remove any valuables from the home and any perishables left in the refrigerator. Secure the residence and take steps to make the home look occupied

5. Stop or forward the mail. This can take a few days to go into effect.

6. Arrange for funeral and burial or cremation.

7. Prepare an obituary.

Within a month after death:

1. Obtain multiple copies of the death certificate.

2. Open a bank account if necessary to pay bills.

3. Contact a trust or estate attorney to transfer assets and assist with probate issues.

4. Take the will to the appropriate county or city office to have it accepted for probate.

5. Contact police, to have them periodically check the house if vacant.

6. Speak with an accountant or tax preparer for estate tax return information.

7. Contact the investment adviser or broker for pertinent financial information.

8. Contact the banker to find accounts and the safe deposit box.

9. Call the insurance agent for life insurance claim forms.

10. Call Social Security and Veteran's Affairs to stop payments and ask about applicable survivor benefits.

11. Call the agency providing pension services for claim forms to stop monthly check.

12. Cancel prescriptions.

13. Transfer car titles.

14. Notify Registrar of Voters.

15. File any outstanding health insurance or Medicare claims.

16. Send acknowledgements for flowers, donations, food, other acts of kindness and pall bearers.

Notes

To die will be an awfully

big adventure.

Peter Pan

Printed in Great Britain
by Amazon